THE BEST BOOK OF

Pirates

Barnaby Harward

KINGFISHER
BOSTON

Contents

KINGFISHER

a Houghton Mifflin Company imprint
222 Berkeley Street
Boston, Massachusetts 02116
www.houghtonmifflinbooks.com

Created for Kingfisher Publications Plc
by Picthall & Gunzi Limited

Author and Editor: Barnaby Harward
Designer: Dominic Zwemmer
Senior Editor: Lauren Robertson
Consultant: Richard Platt

Illustrators: Angus McBride,
John Batchelor, Richard Draper,
Peter Dennis (Linda Rogers Associates),
Christian Hook, Francesca D'Ottavi,
Shirley Tourret

First published in 2002
10 9 8 7 6 5 4
4TR/1104/WKT/MA/128KMA

LIBRARY OF CONGRESS CATALOGING-IN-PUBLICATION DATA
Harward, Barnaby.
  The best book of pirates / by Barnaby Harward.—1st ed.
    p. cm.
  1. Pirates—Juvenile literature. I. Title.

G535 .H34 2002
910.4'5—dc21   2002030421

ISBN 0-7534-5449-1
ISBN 978-07534-5449-7

Printed in China

What are pirates?

Pirates are people who attack and rob ships at sea. They are desperate thieves and cruel murderers. Greek pirates attacked ships in the Mediterranean Sea around 2,700 years ago. One thousand years ago pirates from Scandinavia, called Vikings, sailed the seas of northern Europe. The most famous pirates lived in the 1600s and 1700s.

Corsairs

In the 1500s pirates from North Africa, the corsairs, plundered ships in the Mediterranean Sea. They whipped the slaves who had to row their ships.

Pirates kidnap Caesar

In around 75 B.C., before Julius Caesar became Roman emperor, he was captured by pirates from Turkey. He was held hostage until the Romans paid the pirates a huge ransom.

Privateers

François le Clerc was a French privateer in the 1500s. Privateers were pirates sent by their government to rob enemy ships when their country was at war. Le Clerc had a wooden leg and was known as *Jambe de Bois*, which means "peg leg" in French.

Buccaneers

The buccaneers were pirates who lived on the Caribbean island of Hispaniola. In the 1600s they attacked Spanish ships loaded with treasure as they sailed from South America back to Spain. In time buccaneers took over other Caribbean islands, and then they sailed all over the world.

Buccaneers on the island of Hispaniola

5

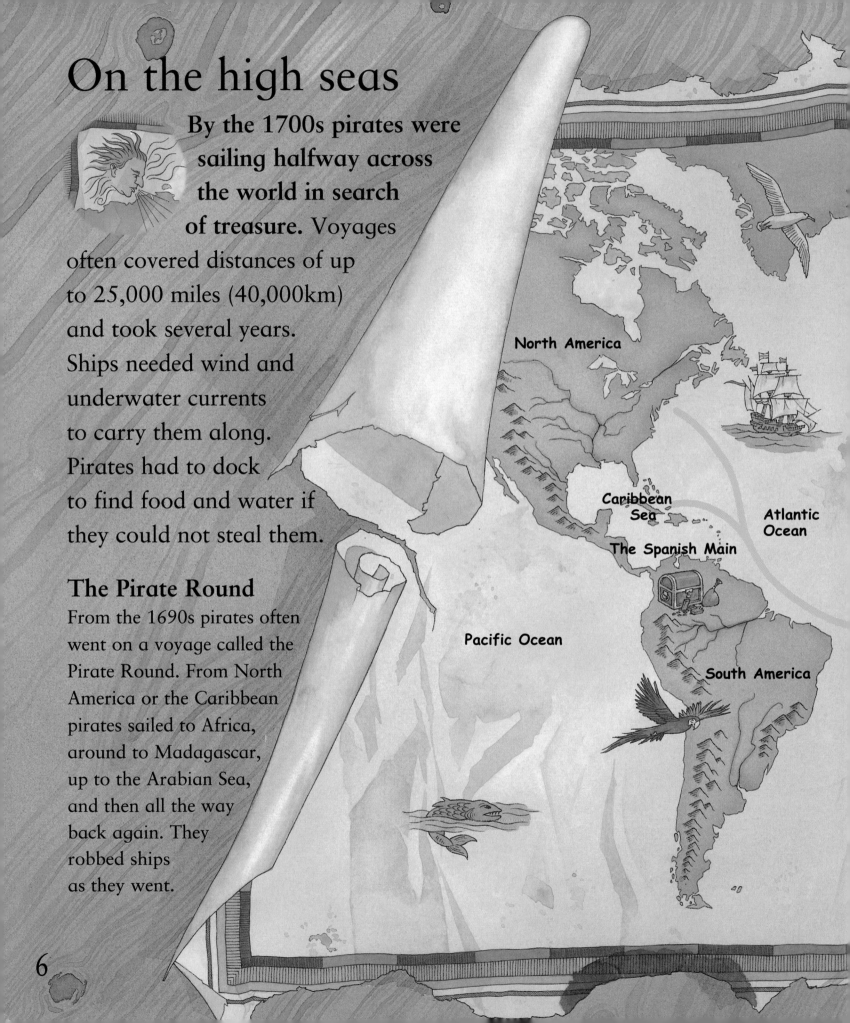

On the high seas

By the 1700s pirates were sailing halfway across the world in search of treasure. Voyages often covered distances of up to 25,000 miles (40,000km) and took several years. Ships needed wind and underwater currents to carry them along. Pirates had to dock to find food and water if they could not steal them.

The Pirate Round

From the 1690s pirates often went on a voyage called the Pirate Round. From North America or the Caribbean pirates sailed to Africa, around to Madagascar, up to the Arabian Sea, and then all the way back again. They robbed ships as they went.

North America

Caribbean Sea

Atlantic Ocean

The Spanish Main

Pacific Ocean

South America

A pirate ship

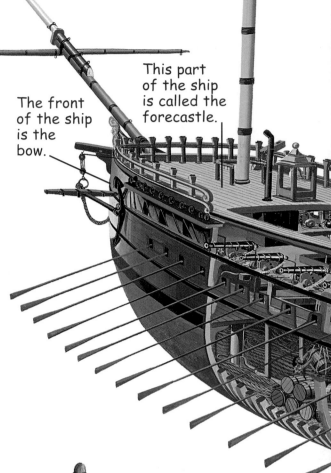

Pirates liked ships that were small and fast. They often stole ships and sometimes altered them to make them go faster or carry more guns. Small ships were useful because they could sail into shallow water and hide up rivers and creeks. Keeping a wooden ship in good condition was hard work. Every pirate had to know how to repair the sails and keep the ship waterproof.

The front of the ship is the bow.

This part of the ship is called the forecastle.

Bartholomew Roberts

Christopher Moody

Blackbeard

Henry Avery

John "Calico Jack" Rackham

Thomas Tew

8

The ship's 34 cannons fired cannonballs weighing 12 lbs (5.4kg) each.

Sailors turn the capstan to lift the anchor.

The captain's cabin

The *Adventure Galley*

Captain William Kidd's ship was called the *Adventure Galley*. It was built in 1695, and Kidd sailed it to the Indian Ocean in 1696. The ship was abandoned on Madagascar because it leaked badly.

The back of the ship is the stern.

Sailors used oars to power the galley when there was no wind.

Barrels full of drinking water

The rudder steers the ship.

The ship's anchor weighed nearly 3,100 lbs (1,400kg).

Pirate flags

A pirate's flag was called a *Jolly Roger*. Not all flags had only a skull and crossbones on them. Pirate captains designed their flags to frighten their enemies. There are many different ones.

Christopher Condent

9

All aboard!

Life on board a pirate ship was tough, and the ships were uncomfortable. In calm weather, when the ship could not move, pirates passed the time drinking rum or gambling. They were usually drunk, and fights often broke out. There was no medicine, and most ships did not have doctors. Pirates who were sick or injured in battle usually died.

The right course

It is difficult to find your way at sea. Pirates used all kinds of instruments to help them navigate. Compasses, maps, and telescopes were useful tools, and pirates often stole them from other ships.

Dinnertime

It was hard to keep food fresh aboard a pirate ship. Salt was added to meat to make it last. Pirates ate crackers called hard tack, which were often infested with weevils. If they ran out of food, the pirates had to eat the rats that lived on the ship.

A pirate climbs the rigging to check on the sails.

Chickens were kept on the ship for eggs and meat.

Pirates sometimes caught fish to eat.

Knowing how to tie knots was important for every sailor.

Tools of the trade

A pirate's trade was piracy, and the tools of his trade were his weapons. Guns and swords were as valuable to him as any treasure. Pirates always made sure that their weapons were in good working order. In a battle their lives depended on them. The most famous pirate weapon was the cutlass, a short razor-sharp sword.

Cannon fire

In the 1500s pirate ships began to use cannons to shoot at enemy ships. The gunpowder used in the cannons was dangerous, and there were many accidents.

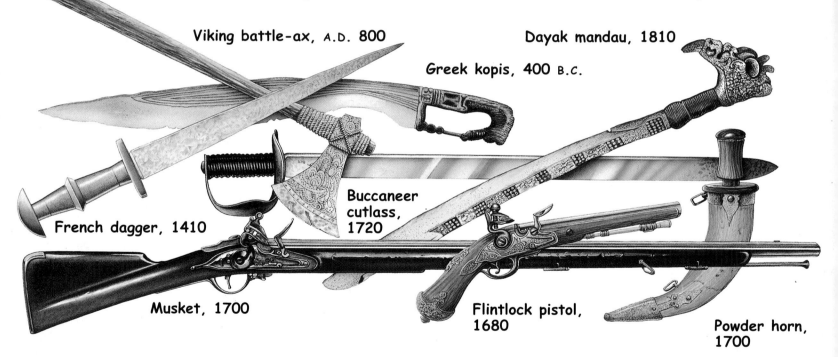

Viking battle-ax, A.D. 800

Greek kopis, 400 B.C.

Dayak mandau, 1810

French dagger, 1410

Buccaneer cutlass, 1720

Musket, 1700

Flintlock pistol, 1680

Powder horn, 1700

Pirate weapons

Pirates used many different weapons. The Vikings used battle-axes. The Greeks used a short sword called a kopis. The Dayaks from Borneo had swords called mandaus. The buccaneers used cutlasses, pistols, and muskets. Pistols and daggers were the easiest weapons to use on board a ship.

Hand-to-hand combat

When pirates sailed alongside
another ship, they jumped
aboard and fought on deck.
If they won the battle, the
pirates stole anything that
they found on board and
sometimes even stole
the ship as well.

The Barbary pirates

Five hundred years ago the north coast of Africa was called the Barbary Coast.
The pirates who came from this area were Muslims and were called Barbary corsairs. They attacked many Christian ships in the Mediterranean Sea, and they captured Christians and sold them as slaves. Important people were held for ransom. The corsairs also forced Christians to row their galleys.

Barbarossa brothers

The two most famous corsairs were the brothers Arouj and Khair-ed-Din. They were nicknamed "Barbarossa," which means red beard.
In 1504 Arouj stole two treasure ships that belonged to the Pope.

Arouj Barbarossa opening a chest on the Pope's treasure ship

Turning Turk

Some Christians "turned Turk," or became Muslims, when the corsairs captured them. This meant that they did not have to become slaves. Englishman Sir Francis Verney and Dutchman Simon Danziger "turned Turk" and became Barbary corsairs themselves.

Sir Francis Verney

Slaves for sale

Christian pirates sold Muslims as slaves, just like the Barbary corsairs who sold Christians as slaves. One of the biggest slave markets in Europe was on the island of Malta in the Mediterranean Sea.

15

The Spanish Main

After the European discovery of the Americas in 1492 the Spanish frequently sailed there. The lands they visited were called the Spanish Main. They stole treasures from the Aztecs, who lived in what is now called Mexico. The treasure was carried back to Spain in ships called galleons. Pirates and privateers attacked these ships on their way home.

Queen of England's favorite pirate

Sir Francis Drake was an English explorer and privateer. He attacked and robbed Spanish ships when England was at war with Spain in the 1570s and 1580s. In 1581 he was knighted by Queen Elizabeth I.

Jean Fleury's prize

Three Spanish galleons loaded with treasure from the Spanish Main were attacked by the French privateer Jean Fleury in 1523. He captured two of them but one escaped.

Galleons floated high in the water, which made them easier to load and unload than some other ships.

The platform high up on the mast is called the crow's nest and was used as a lookout.

Blackbeard braided his beard with rope, which he would set on fire to frighten his enemies.

18

Piracy in the Caribbean

The Caribbean Sea attracted many pirates who hoped to rob Spanish treasure ships.

The pirates who lived on the island of Hispaniola were called buccaneers. They got their name from the fire on which they smoked and dried meat. This was called a *boucan* or *buccan*. Buccaneers began attacking Spanish ships in the 1630s.

Morgan's raids

Onc of the greatest buccaneers was Henry Morgan. He raided Spanish ports and towns in the 1660s and 1670s and became rich. In 1674 he was appointed the deputy governor of Jamaica by the King of England.

Blackbeard

The most famous pirate of all was Blackbeard. He attacked ships and ports up and down the east coast of the Americas. He was a huge man, and everyone was afraid of him— even his own crew.

African coasts

Pirates from Europe and the Americas sailed to Africa in search of gold, ivory, and slaves. They bought slaves along Africa's Guinea Coast to sell in the Americas. Slaves were valuable cargo but were treated badly and sold like animals. The nearby island of Madagascar was also popular with pirates. Many of them lived there between 1690 and 1723.

Pirates cleaning barnacles and seaweed off the bottom, or hull, of a ship

Careening a ship

Madagascar was a safe place for pirates. They went there to clean and repair their ships. When a ship is careened, it is taken out of the water so its hull can be cleaned. Pirates scrubbed the hull so that the ship could move faster in the water.

Bartholomew Roberts

The Welshman, Bartholomew Roberts, was one of the most successful pirates. He was a cruel man, and he made a lot of money buying and selling slaves. By the time he was killed in 1722, he had captured or sunk over 400 ships off the African and Caribbean coasts.

Roberts wore a diamond cross, which he may have stolen from the King of Portugal.

The Orient

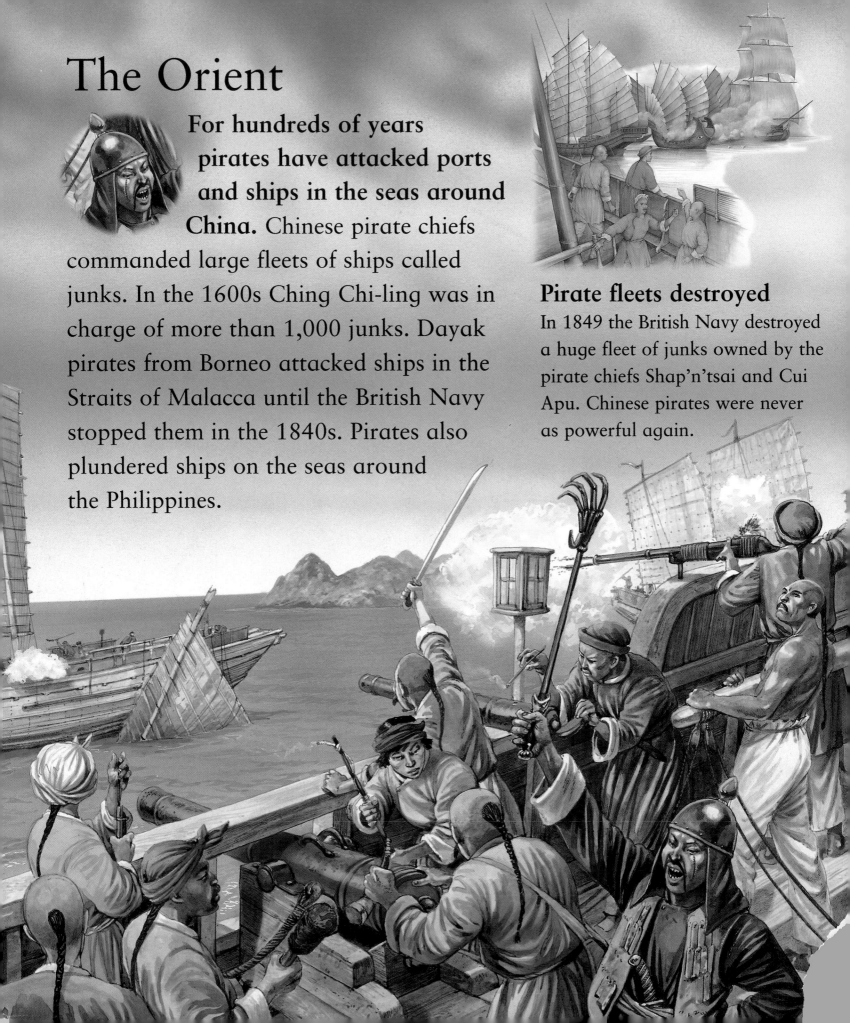

For hundreds of years pirates have attacked ports and ships in the seas around China. Chinese pirate chiefs commanded large fleets of ships called junks. In the 1600s Ching Chi-ling was in charge of more than 1,000 junks. Dayak pirates from Borneo attacked ships in the Straits of Malacca until the British Navy stopped them in the 1840s. Pirates also plundered ships on the seas around the Philippines.

Pirate fleets destroyed

In 1849 the British Navy destroyed a huge fleet of junks owned by the pirate chiefs Shap'n'tsai and Cui Apu. Chinese pirates were never as powerful again.

Madame Cheng

When the pirate chief Cheng I died in 1807, his wife took control of his fleet. Soon Madame Cheng commanded 1,800 junks and boats and 80,000 pirates. She was captured by the Chinese government in 1810, but she paid them to set her free, and she became a smuggler.

Madame Cheng and her crew attacking other Chinese junks

Pirate women

Women were usually not allowed on pirate ships, but some still managed to become pirates. They had to pretend they were men by dressing and fighting like men. Some pirate women were even braver and stronger than the men on their ships. A few pirate women, such as Madame Cheng, became very powerful.

The pirate princess
Alwilda was a Swedish princess who lived more than 1,200 years ago. Her father tried to force her to marry a prince. She did not like the man her father had chosen, so she became a pirate.

Anne Bonny came from Ireland and was married to a sailor before she became a pirate.

The Irish lady

Grace O'Malley was an Irish noblewoman who commanded a fleet of pirate galleys in the 1500s. Her pirates attacked ships in the Atlantic Ocean. Unlike most pirates, she lived into old age. She died in 1603 when she was 73 years old.

Grace O'Malley lived on the west coast of Ireland.

Before joining Rackham's ship, Mary Read was a soldier in the British Army.

"Calico Jack's" women

Anne Bonny and Mary Read sailed on "Calico Jack" Rackham's ship. The ship was captured by the British Navy in 1720, and all the men were executed. The two women could not be executed because they claimed they were pregnant.

25

Buried treasure

There are many stories about pirates burying treasure, but we do not know whether these stories are true. Grace O'Malley is said to have buried many tons of gold and jewels. Captain Kidd actually buried his treasure on Gardiner's Island off Long Island, New York. In reality most pirates spent their money as soon as they got it or lost it through gambling. Pirates not only stole treasure— they also stole goods that they could sell.

Henry Avery
In 1695 Henry Avery and his pirates captured a vast treasure ship belonging to the Indian emperor. Later Avery lost all his money and died a poor man.

Captain Kidd buried his treasure on Gardiner's Island.

Kidd turns to piracy
Captain Kidd sailed to the Indian Ocean to arrest Henry Avery, but instead became a pirate himself. Kidd was caught and his treasure dug up. He was executed in London in 1701.

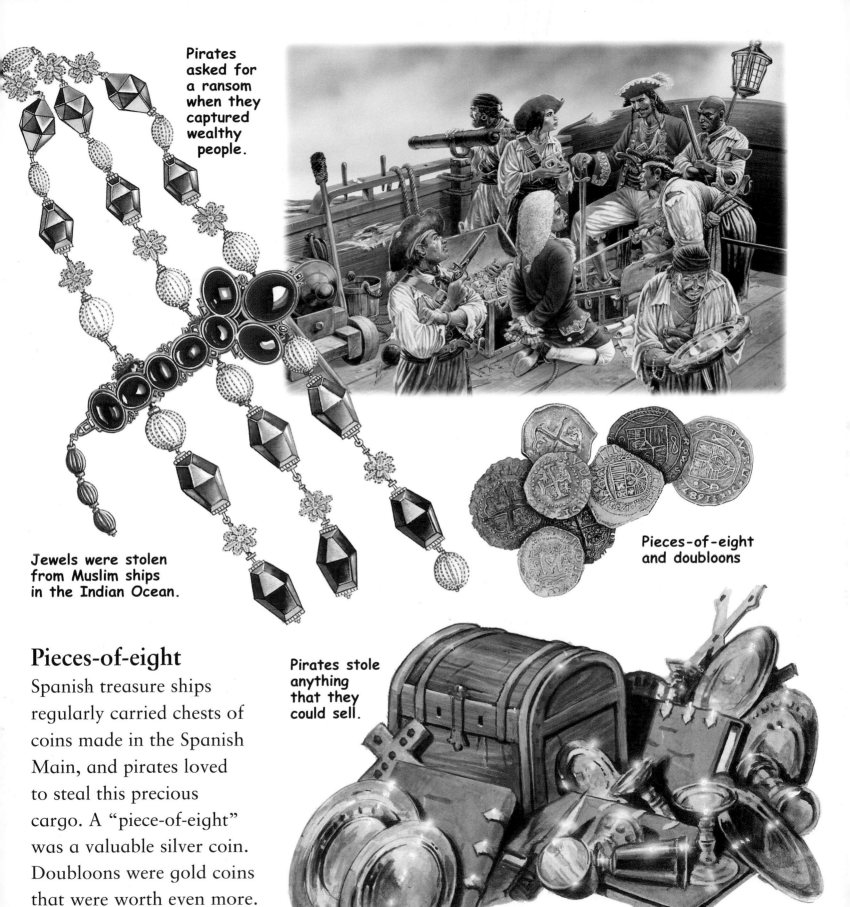

Pirates asked for a ransom when they captured wealthy people.

Jewels were stolen from Muslim ships in the Indian Ocean.

Pieces-of-eight and doubloons

Pieces-of-eight

Spanish treasure ships regularly carried chests of coins made in the Spanish Main, and pirates loved to steal this precious cargo. A "piece-of-eight" was a valuable silver coin. Doubloons were gold coins that were worth even more.

Pirates stole anything that they could sell.

Rules of the game

Most pirate captains forced the pirates on their ships to follow a set of rules. These were strict, but they were also fair. There were rules about how treasure should be shared and rules about how crimes should be punished. For the worst crimes, the punishment was execution. Men were thrown overboard to drown or be eaten by sharks. Walking the plank was not a common punishment.

Sharing the loot
Treasure and stolen goods were divided among the crew of a pirate ship. The captain and other important people usually took a larger share than the crew.

Marooned
Any pirate caught stealing from another pirate was marooned. This meant he was left on an island with only a pistol, some gunpowder, and a small supply of drinking water.

A marooned pirate sits on a beach as his ship sails away.

The pirate has enough drinking water to last for two or three days.

29

Pirates of today

There are not as many pirates today as there were in the 1700s, but recently pirate attacks have become more common. Modern pirates attack ships in the Indian Ocean and South China Sea. They also rob luxury yachts in the Caribbean and the Mediterranean seas. In 1998 a supertanker was captured by Chinese pirates and was not found for two weeks.

Pirates about to attack a container ship

Night attack
Modern pirates use speedboats, and they carry knives and machine guns. They usually attack small container ships and steal as much cargo as they can as well as valuables from the captain's safe.

Glossary

cargo Everything a ship carries that will be sold when it arrives at its destination.

crew The people, led by the ship's captain, who work on a ship.

cutlass A short sword. Cutlasses were the buccaneers' favorite weapons.

execute To put someone to death because the law demands it. Execution is a punishment for serious crimes.

fleet A large group of ships commanded by one person.

galleon A large sailing ship with three or more masts.

galley A ship that is powered by oars as well as sails.

gamble To bet money on dice or card games.

gunpowder A powder that causes an explosion when it is lit.

Pirates used gunpowder in cannons and to make bombs.

hostage A person who is taken, or kidnapped, and held prisoner by pirates or other criminals. A hostage is often released when a ransom is paid.

ivory Elephant tusks are made of ivory. It is illegal to kill elephants for their tusks.

junk A type of Chinese ship.

knighted To be given a special position in British society and the title "Sir."

loot Anything that has been stolen, such as treasure or cargo.

musket An old-fashioned type of gun. Modern guns similar to muskets are called rifles.

Muslim A person who follows the religion of Islam.

navigating Working out a route for a ship to sail at sea.

oar A long piece of wood that is pulled back and forth in the water to move a ship. Only small boats use oars today.

plunder To take things by force. Pirates plundered ships and ports.

port A town with a harbor next to a big river or the sea. Ships load and unload cargo at a port.

ransom Money that pirates and other kidnappers ask for in return for a prisoner or hostage.

slave Someone who is captured and sold or made to work for the people who have captured them. Slavery is now against the law in most countries.

smuggler A person who brings things into a country without paying taxes. Smuggling is against the law.

31

Index